Pionus Parrots as Pets

The Ultimate Guide for Pionus Parrots

Pionus Parrots General Info, Purchasing, Care, Cost, Keeping, Health, Supplies, Food, Breeding and More Included!

By Lolly Brown

Foreword

Also known as the red vented parrots, Pionus birds are really smart parrots that are generally playful and would welcome interaction with a familiar face once they get to know the individual. There is also something quietly rewarding about gently playing with a Pionus. There is just something about them that brings out the tranquility within you.

They are gracious housemates who are able to integrate themselves easily into the new homes they join. They are curious investigators of anything new as long as they do not feel threatened or in danger. Providing the Pionus parrots with toys and trinkets will make them happy campers who will quietly go about their day amusing you with their little antics!

Table of Contents

Introduction..1

Chapter One: A Closer Look at Pionus Birds...........3

General Characteristics **4**

Types of Pionus Parrots **6**

Chapter Two: Pionus Parrots as Pets.....................11

Physical and Behavioral Characteristics **12**

Chapter Three: Species and Subspecies of the Pionus Parrots
....17

Blue-headed Pionus **18**

The Ecuadorian Sordid Pionus **19**

The Columbian Sordid Parrot..............................**20**

The Maximilian's Parrot......................................**21**

The Plum-crowned Parrot...................................**22**

The Red-billed Pionus...**24**

Subspecies of Red-billed Pionus.........................**24**

Chapter Four: Purchasing a Healthy Parrot...........27

Cost of Buying a Pionus Parrot Species **28**

Some Reminders Before Acquiring a Pet Parrot **29**

Choosing a Breeder **31**

How to Spot a Healthy Pionus............................**33**

Chapter Five: Nutrition and Feeding 35

Caring for and Feeding Your Pionus 36

Chapter Six: Housing, Bird Rooms and Maintenance 43

Cage Measurements for Pionus Parrots 44

Bird Proofing Rooms 47

Chapter Seven: Temperament and Training 55

Social Behaviors 56

Training and Handling Pionus Parrots 57

Initial Training 57

Advanced Training 58

Playtime Activities 59

Chapter Eight: Grooming Needs and Health Care 61

Importance of Grooming Your Parrot 62

Bird Baths 62

Wings 63

Beak 64

Nails 65

Health Care 66

Chapter Nine: Breeding Your Pionus Parrots 77

Pionus Parrot Sexing 78

Breeding/Reproduction 78

Breeding Environment 79

Egg Laying and Hatchlings 79

Potential Health Problems...80

Life Span and Availability 81

Chapter Ten: Additional Requirements and Summary........85

Quick Summary..86

Bird Housing, Toys, Playpens and other Equipment.....87

Housing and Bird Cages for Different Species 88

Temperatures..88

Health Maintenance...89

Legal Aspects of Owning...90

Tips of How to Spot a Legit Breeder/Bird 91

Glossary of Bird Terms 93

Index...99

Photo Credits...105

References..107

Introduction

Pionus parrots are overlooked species because they seem drab – looking but there's no doubt that these beautiful creatures make great family pets. These parrots are often times mistaken as a smaller version of Amazon parrots because they have lots of similar characteristics. Compared to their Amazon parrot look - alike, Pionus birds are more gentle and docile, though they can be aggressive if not properly socialized but in general they don't have those bold Amazon – ish qualities. Males could also become quite aggressive towards females especially during mating season. These birds bond closely with family members and even if they're not quite talkative they can connect with people.

Speaking of talking, Pionus birds have a soft quality of tone that could be a little raspy sometimes, and if you listen to them closely, you can surely enjoy their attempt in speaking to you even if they can only pick up a few words or only has a limited vocabulary. If you want to have a slightly larger pet bird that won't bother you nor your neighbor, Pionus parrots are perfect companions!

Pionus birds in general don't crave for its owner's attention but just like other bird species or pets they still need constant interaction though they can be quite independent, so just make sure that you provide them with interesting toys for physical and mental stimulation.

The next few chapters and sections will provide you with more information about this species' biological background, its different types, and information on how to acquire them, feed them, groom them and take care of them so that they can be happy companions.

Chapter One: A Closer Look at Pionus Birds

What truly sets them apart and gives them distinction are the red vent feathers all eight species of Pionus share. Another distinct mark of appearance would be their eyes. All eight species share the bare-eye ring that surrounds their eyes. Natives of South and Central America as well as Mexico, the Pionus parrots may not have been the first choice of many parrot lovers in the past, but all that is changing now. Let's find out more about them.

General Characteristics

The smallest of the parrot species, the Pionus bird has been an overlooked pet who actually makes for a great companion for all sorts of individuals but more especially so for those who are not that into talkers. These robustly stocky birds with are small look-alikes of their cousin the Amazon. But unlike the Amazon, whose colors can be stark, vivid and almost high-definition to look at, the colors of the more petite Pionus is more iridescent, like a shimmering gleans of rainbow colors passing under the sun.

The Pionus parrot, with a speckle-faced appearance is generally classified under a two-specie category with a minute number of authorities suggesting that the blue-headed parrot be categorically separated into two or three species.

These parrots, rare as some of them may be, are becoming more popular bird pets for many avian lovers. These little mostly-green bodied parrots have been noted to be really good home companions for the family because of its mild demeanor. The Dusky Pionus, a native of Surinam, also found in the mountainous regions of South America and Guyana, has become more common in the pet trade largely owing to captive breeding. Unlike the Amazon parrots, our focus the Pionus parrots is a quieter flock. Aviculturists have noted that as compared to some other pet parrots, Pionus parrots are not all that energetic, and that they do not like or appreciate hands-on play like being turned over on their backs. However, they do make for good quiet roomies and companions. Pionus parrots are also noted to have been described by owners as charming and gentle pets.

Birds of this genus emit a characteristic wheezing or snorting sound when it is frightened or excited. This is mistaken sometimes for a symptom of disease or a sign of distress. They emit a sweet odor or a musky one, which a few caretakers find to be unpleasant, but others seem to enjoy. In captivity, Pionus parrots are prone to aspergillosis, vitamin A deficiency, and obesity. With the exception of aspergillosis, these conditions can be easily prevented with proper owner care.

Generally, the Pionus parrots as a species, eats food naturally available and found in its natural habitat. Its diet is mostly made up of fruits, showing better preference for (or availability of) guavas. Raising them in captivity, bird owners should take care not to feed their birds any sort of high-fat foods to stave off the tendency to and development of obesity and other medical issues related to being overweight.

Many pet shops usually sell banana chips fried in oil to make them crispy and given to some birds as treats. For many other birds this could be good snacks, however fried banana chips have too much fatty components for the pionus parrot and the bird may result in high cholesterol or other related health issues due to excessive fat intake. Owners of pionus parrots have to get the services of and consult with a South American exotic bird expert or a veterinarian knowledgeable on the proper dietary needs of the Pionus parrot.

Types of Pionus Parrots

There are many Pionus parrots and each of them has their own distinctive color but all of them share these basic appearances. We shall discuss the differences of these parrots further.

The Pionus menstruus

The Pionus menstruus or the Blue-headed parrot is predominantly green. One of the quietest in the spectrum, the blue-headed sort, as it name suggests has a blue head and neck. It has red undertail coverts and is found in the tropical areas of both South and Central America.

The Pionus sordidus

The Pionus sordidus or the red-billed parrot is predominantly green. The color and appearance of the red-bill's chest is dull blue and a bright red bill. It has a red undertail coverts and commonly found in the north-western regions of South America

The Pionus maximiliani

The Pionus maximiliani or the scaly-headed parrot stands out with a green head of feathers and is trimmed in a royal blue. The color of the chest of the scaly-headed parrot can range anywhere from royal blue to indigo. Its wings and back are mostly green in hue and some birds could develop, on their shoulders, bronze 'epaulets'. The bird's vent area has a red undertail. In this area, feathers are tipped with a hue of light green and in other bird's aqua or violet. The color of its beak could range anywhere from horn to black in color, with most birds sporting two-tone beak colors. The skin color of the Pionus typically ranges from grey to pink. The scaly-headed of the Maximiliani comes from eastern and central South America

The Pionus senilis

The Pionus senilis or the white-crowned parrot is typically seen to be dark blue and dark green with a white crown, white forehead, and a whitish throat. It usually has an olive-colored patch on its shoulder. The white-crowned parrot has a light green belly with a shock of red undertail coverts. Both female and males could have a pinkish ring around its eyes. The white-crowned parrot hails from Mexico and Central America.

The Pionus tumultuosus

The Pionus tumultuosus or the speckle-faced parrot is predominantly green with a muted bluish-grey colored neck with red undertail coverts. Its head is either speckled red or white and calls the Andes in South America, home.

The Pionus chalcopterus

The Pionus chalcopterus or the bronze-winged parrot has a dark blue body with red undertail coverts. It has a pinkish throat with dark bronze-green wings and it natural habitat can be found in the north-western regions of South America.

The Pionus fuscus

The Pionus fuscus or the dusky parrot has a dark brownish-grey body. Its flight feathers are the color blue and its undertail coverts are red. The Dusky parrot is native to north-eastern regions of South America.

Chapter Two: Pionus Parrots as Pets

There are not too many people who consider Pionus parrots to keep as pets, passing them over for a more interactive, talkative, more colorful parrot, but this is their allure. Since many have passed up opportunities of sharing home with Pionus parrots, fanciers have found them compellingly intriguing Pionus owners are few and far between and usually chance upon each other on the Internet. Generally, the Pionus is known to be an easy-going, slightly-standoffish, quiet, mid-sized bird. In reality, these descriptions of its personality and traits are based on comparisons to the more popular pet parrot species. The Pionus is indeed quiet when compared to the Macaw, Conure and Amazon. It is quite easy-going compared to African greys and lovebirds.

Physical and Behavioral Characteristics

The length of Pionus parrots, from top of crown to feet ranges from 10 to 12 inches and the all usually share the same body shape as well as short, square-tipped tail just like the Amazon parrots. All Pionus parrots have fleshy eye areas that are bare of feathers with an eye-ring that circles the whole eye of the parrot. All of them also have shared the same red body feathers as well as a red undertail or vent.

This species of Pionus parrots, are considered "drab" in color when compared to other more colorful, more flashy, more talkative and other more commonly kept pet parrots. They may not the most sought after in terms of pet companionship but there are many qualities about it that bird fanciers find fascinating and may just suit your kind of companion and lifestyle need.

The Pionus and the feisty Amazon parrot share many similarities save for the smaller shape-size of the Pionus to the much bigger Amazon. The Pionus is devoted and quiet and not as talkative as an African grey parrot. This parrot sort is not as flashy or vivid like other Conures but is just as compact in size.

All of the eight species of Pionus parrots can be found in a wide range of areas in South and Central America. These parrots tend to inhabit mountainous regions, forested areas, and savannahs. You will observe the Pionus parrot to be a typically hardy eater. These parrots should be given a formulated main diet along with lots of fresh fruit and vegetables.

The Pionus is a little aloof when compared to cockatoos. However, aficionados of these birds who have discovered traits about them tell a different story of these parrots. Although not total love-sponges, Pionus parrots show a measure of affection toward their humans. Although not silent, they are quieter than other parrots as well as they are attentive and sweet. Much like with all parrots, the manner of how a Pionus is raised by its human caregivers make the difference between a great companion and a shy bird. The owner of a Pionus must be prepared to spend a good amount of time with their parrot.

All species of the Pionus parrots, In general, make for a good family bird, and does not tend to developing as a "one person" bird, though this varies by individual. Keep an eye out for children around the birds and do not leave them alone and unsupervised with each other, even though the bite of the Pionus isn't as formidable as the Amazon's or the cockatoo's. Most birds when frightened will either try to flee, bite, or they stand utterly still and unmoving. The Pionus does these as a defense mechanism to live another day. Another interesting survival technique of the Pionus parrot is that it hisses in short bursts, much like it is having trouble catching its breath. One other parrot specie, the Cockatiels, makes similar-sounding noises as well when frightened. Some owners of this bird species have also observed that their parrots give off a sweet, musky scent.

Quite the novelty and a far cry from other parrots, the Pionus is a refreshing diversity from the "everyday" parrot. It's not a relationship not to be taken lightly of done on a whim because a Pionus parrot has been noted to be able to live between 25-40 years if properly cared for!

Pionus aren't known to be the best talkers; however some of them can collect a pretty impressive vocabulary. Not always crystal clear, their "speaking voice" is often described as a little raspy. Most guardians can generally understand what the bird is saying though.

Not much of the talker or noise-maker, the Pionus does make a funny sound that seems to be triggered when it feels frightened, gets startled or disturbed. A wheezing sound emitted by any other bird or parrot would strike a bird lovers heart cold with fear.

Health wise, most parrots are susceptible to aspergillosis, and when affected with this they make a wheezing noise but not so much for the Pionus. This is why it is really important to get to know your Pionus traits and behavioral habits because you will have to tell if it is actually sick or if the bird was simply caught unawares. As much as it is not as prone to aspergillosis, Pionus parrots could still contract this infection if not careful. Avoid using cobs of corn to line its nest because this bedding material has been discovered to harbor this fungal infection and breed spores which proliferates in its abdominal tract when swallowed by the parrot.

Chapter Three: Species and Subspecies of the Pionus Parrots

We will be taking a detailed look at each of the Pionus parrot in this chapter to give you a wider range of their individuality and uniqueness. We aim to help you get to the matter of making a decision on which pionus parrot suits you best, would fit into your lifestyle and even give you a better understanding of each in case you are looking to expand your aviary. Get to know a little more about what they look like, their habitat in nature, when they breed and all the individual details of each pionus specie and sub specie giving lengthier details on the most popular pionus birds available and commonly found in the bird pet market.

Blue-headed Pionus

Let's take a better look at one of the most popular bird species of the Pionus parrots called the Blue-headed Pionus. This sought after parrot from the pinus genus is inquisitive, intelligent, and active. Even though the blue-headed pionus aren't good at talking like most parrots in general, but they make up for this lack of chatter with their fun antics and friendly disposition.

The Blue-headed Pionus are naturally gentle birds and they could potentially turn into a very loyal pet, oftentimes fiercely bonding to their owner. For a beginning parrot owner, the blue-headed pionus are considered to be excellent birds, since they are typically quiet and calm. And because of this, they are also a great pet choice for those who live in apartments or dorms. The scientific name of the blue-headed parrot is Pionus menstruus with sub-species individually called the Pionus menstruus reichenowi and Pionus menstruus rubrigularis. They are birds native in Central America specifically in Costa Rica as well as South America, northern Bolivia and central Brazil. They are also found on Trinidad. They like to inhabit wooded forests as much as they like being in tropical zones.

A small to relatively medium sized species, the blue-headed Pionus has a charming characteristic and has the appearance similar to its other pionus cousins. The bird sports a green plumage and typically varies from the rest of the pionus because it has a bright blue colored - head, sleek black feathers and a splash of pink feathers on its throat.

The Blue-headed Pionus comes to its full colouration when it reaches maturity, and when it does its beautiful feathers has a shimmering quality to it. You will also notice a distinct difference in its fur color. Some appear to have a darkish blue splash of color on the head and a mute or stark pink color on its throat. The blue-headed pionus like all its cousins have bright feathers of red for its undertail. The bird's beak is dark grey and transitions to red higher up toward its head, it also has dark brown eyes with a light grey colored on its eye ring, and their legs are pale greenish-grey. The young pionus have even paler bluish coloring on their heads as compared to the adults. They grow to a length of 11" (28 cm). It is relatively a robust bird, but more susceptible to the infection aspergillosis than other species. Availability of this parrot is infrequent but is becoming more popular and many are known to be kept as pets.

The Ecuadorian Sordid Pionus

The Pionus sordidus mindorensis or the Ecuadorian Sordid Parrots call the Mountains of western Ecuador home. The Ecuadorian Sordid Parrots' head is a dull slate-blue in color with lores (areas between eyes and bill on the side of the bird's head are red with black ear-coverts, edged with whitish feathers. It has chin feathers that is edged with dull pink and its back and wings are a dark brown color with pale edging on each feather. The breast and abdomen of the Ecuadorian is brown with dull pink sometimes bluish edging.

It has a violet-blue color on it's under wing-coverts. It has a dark blue tail with outer feathers of a red base. Its bill is blackish, and horn-colored on the sides. The have brown iris and feet grey and measures in at a length of 10 in (26 cm). The Ecuadorian Sordid comes from the mountains of western Ecuador.

The Columbian Sordid Parrot

Columbian Sordid Parrot averages a length of 11 inches (28 cm). The Colombian Sordid parrot looks much like the parrot mentioned, described and featured above, but is overall a darker green in color without olive-brown markings on the back feathers. Its breast and abdomen is a uniform green, sans the bluish-pink edging. This parrot subspecies of the pionus is generally found in the regions of the Santa Marta Mountains in northern Columbia.

The Maximilian's Parrot

This Pionus sort appears quite plain when observed from a distance but like the Dusky Parrot; the Maximilian has a variety of soft colors that are stunningly beautiful when seen in full sunlight. It is also called the Scaly-headed Parrot because the feathers on its head have grey edges giving it a scaly appearance. They are found over the regions of eastern South America from north Brazil to Bolivia, Paraguay, and Argentina. They like to inhabit lowland forests and open woodlands.

The one who calls Surinam and Guyana their native habitat, the Dusky Pionus, has also gained better recognition and following largely because of captive breeding. Loved for their subdued hues that have an iridescent appearance under direct sunshine and its ability to pick up and retain teachings. They are very curious, smart and have very good memories. When they learn a trait like stepping up, they are quite obedient and will remain steadfast in their training. It has one of the nicest pet bird personalities and is an ideal pet for first-time parrot owners. They also make wonderful family pets because they can be handed by more than one person and still keep their sweet disposition. It makes for a suitable pet for those who dwell in apartments because you will hardly hear a peep from them that would cause alarm or a fuss.

The Plum-crowned Parrot

The speckle-faced or the Plum-crowned pious has the same predominantly green body and red undertail vent much like the rest of the Pionus species. It also shares the bare eye rings the other Pionus sorts have as well. What set each of them apart from each other would be the subdued colors that are unique to each and that make them easily identifiable to the trained eye. The appearance of the plum-crowned parrot is a little more colorful than usual what with its head full of dark red feathers, highlighted at the tips with splashes of purple along with areas of white feathers (giving it the name speckle-face). The plum-crowned Pionus typically would have either a yellow or olive-colored bill or eyes of brown, its nape and back feathered in black. They are found to favor high-altitude parts as well as densely forested areas. When they do "speak" and make bird-call noises, the speckle-faced or plum-crowned Pionus emits a sound resembling or closely sounding like a laugh.

Plum-crowned parrots are said to be nervous and skittish in the wild as well as in captivity. Perhaps because of this trait it is virtually nonexistent in aviculture with exception to one small, private collection in the United States and another at the Loro Parque Fundación.

Most of the plum-crowned parrots imported into the United States fall and has fallen victims to aspergillosis perhaps brought on about by the stress when transported. They begin to breed during between November and December and the young fledge in February/March. During mating season, the Plum-crowned Parrots are frequently observed to flock in small groups. They camouflage well in the foliage, are quiet and approachable when they forage and other times, alert and evasive.

They sound similar to the Red-billed Pionus (Pionus seniloides) and the noises they make to call-out. Their call-sounds are described to be distinctive. When frightened, they screech loudly as they take flight. Call-outs made in flight are clear notes of a laughing quality which may also sound harsher sometimes. They emit nasal tones when perched. Spring in the US signals the breeding period for the plum-crowns.

These parrots are particularly vocal during the morning, is an energetic bird considered to be medium-noisy. Initially, they are flighty and shy and pants with fear when alarmed. It is also slow to trust. Rare parrots, like the plum-crowns, is better left alone in the wild or placed into a well-managed conservation or breeding program to ensure long-term survival. Breeding plum-crowns is seldom achieved in captivity. Birds that are newly imported are very susceptible to diseases and frequent deaths attest to this. They are particularly prone to serious aspergillosis infections.

Plum-crowns are often intolerant of the presence of other birds, so it is best to keep pairs in their flights. They are not hard chewers but it is strongly suggested that you install double wiring to protect birds in adjoining cages. Provide them daily bathing opportunities by outfitting their enclosure with a bath or shower as they enjoy this activity very much.

The Red-billed Pionus

The Sordid Parrot or Pionus sordidus sordidus or the Red-billed Pionus Parrot is native to Northern South America, particularly Venezuela in Lara and Falcón Provinces. Its ubspecie the Columbian Sordid Parrot (Pionus sordidus saturatus) is endemic to the Santa Marta Mountains in northern Columbia.

Subspecies of Red-billed Pionus

The Pionus sordidus corallinus or Coral-billed Pionus or Coral-billed Parrot hails from the Eastern Andes in Colombia, as well as regions in eastern Ecuador, Peru, and northern Bolivia. Coral-billed Pionus aka Coral-billed Parrot aka Red-billed Pionus has a similar appearance to the described and featured previously but its plumage is generally without pale edging. Its head feathers are edged with blue coloration and it has back feathers with a tinge of grey with murky blue tips. It has a breast band of violet-blue with dark edging on its upper wing-coverts. It is also bigger in length, measuring in at 30 cm (12 in), wing length 187 - 206 mm (7.5 - 8 in). The coral-billed pionus subspecies comes from the Eastern Andes in Colombia, as well as regions in eastern Ecuador, Peru, and northern Bolivia.

The Pionus sordidus antelius or the Paler Red-billed Parrot came from the mountains of north-eastern Venezuela. The Perijá Red-billed Parrot or the Pionus sordidus ponsi or the Perijá Red-billed Parrot comes from the general region of the Sierra de Perijá, a chain mountainous forest land that forms the border between northwest Venezuela and northern Columbia.

On average the Red-billed Parrot is about 11 inches (28 cm) in length with a generally olive-green plumage. Its head is likewise olive-green only its feathers to the crown and down the back of its head are edged broadly with dark-blue feathers. It has olive cheeks with blue tips. It has a blue ring across the throat to its upper breast.

The breast and abdomen of the red-billed pionus is dull olive with each feather sporting a duller edging of a bluish-pink tinge. As with other pionus parrots they usually have under tail-coverts of red. It has a dull olive-green back with olive-brown markings. The tail-feathers in the middle are green and outer feathers are blue with a hint of red at the base. It has a red bill with a pale base. The eye rings of the red-billed pionus are grey and its irises dark brown. They have grey feet. Juvenile birds sport a pale green head, a yellowish-green undertail with a few red feathers.

Chapter Four: Purchasing a Healthy Parrot

Before you close any deals you will want to ask questions and get upfront answers. Getting an ill bird can pose a bigger problem that can be harmful to humans. You will want to determine the origin of the birds. You should never try to purchase a bird from overseas because it is primarily illegal and any bird getting into a market could potentially be a carrier of diseases that could cause outbreaks.

Cost of Buying a Pionus Parrot Species

Be sure to set realistic expectations about how much money you want to spend, determine the amount of money you can afford to spend and do not deviate from it. A Pionus depending on its specie, availability, and rarity will cost anywhere from $200 to a whopping $900. The White-capped is one of the most popular pet choices and a Pionus that doesn't demand such an exorbitant price in the pet trade costing anywhere from $200 to $400. A far cry from the more rare Pionus parrots which are more challenging to breed in captivity like the Bronze-winged Pionus can cost up to a $900 tab upon purchase.

If you are looking to adopt or rescue a Pionus you will want to get an idea of how old it is for purposes of; updating or creating a fresh medical record, diet needs and breeding possibilities. Determining the age of an adult Pionus is easy to look for because it would have been tagged with specific ink marking banded around its leg. This would depend on whether the bird was initially registered early on in its life.

Some Reminders Before Acquiring a Pet Parrot

Any responsibly thoughtful pet owner will make it a point to get to know the pet they would want to care for. This shows a level of maturity and readiness for the commitment of taking in an animal to raise and be companion. Consider your finances early and figure out the math on the initial acquisition as well as the monthly and yearly costs to set expectations straight and to not get in over your head have a budget and stick to it.

A Blue-Headed and Maximillian Pionus is the kind you want to consider if you want a chatty parrot for companion. It is true that the pionus is perhaps the quietest of all parrots, and not all of them can be trained to talk except the Blue-Headed and Maximilian species! It may take a while to train your Pionus to learn how to speak, but these are the species that can eventually learn lots of phrases. Choose a Maximillian Pionus if you aren't fond of a parrot that screech. The meek Maximillian is the quietest of all the Pionus parrots species and is not averse to squawking and screeching. Living in close proximity with your neighbors like in an apartment will get you concerned about disturbing them. If you intend to keep peaceful relations with the folks next door then you can be rest assured that this is the species to care for.

If you fancy bright, more vibrant colors think about raising a Blue-Headed parrot if you preferred vibrant colors. The bluish feathers on its head, gives the bird that classic "parrot look" which makes the Blue-Headed parrot the most popular species of pionus species. In addition to this burst of blue they also sport bright pink, sometimes red, feathers underneath their tail.

Generally, all juvenile pionus birds sport less color as compared to mature ones. As these birds mature into adulthood, they will begin to develop their subtle hues and bright splotches of rich colors best enjoyed and observed in bright sunlight. Maximillian Pionus species are usually sought after and selected by bird lovers because of its ability to socialize easily. Most Pionus species can be a tad shy at the beginning but they have been observed to be independent so it is important to allow the bird to get to know you by spending time - and sharing space with it frequently. It terms of socialization, the Maximillian is the Pionus that is most tolerant of interaction both with humans and other feathered aviators. They are quite happy to share a home with other birds and can get along with them splendidly.

Choosing a Breeder

You must take time to set an appointment with a list of prepared questions relevant to the care and husbandry of the birds you intend to bring home. Below are some tips:

- When dealing with breeders of the Pionus, you want to walk away with the assurance of a guarantee. No exceptions. If a breeder cannot give you some sort of guarantee you will just have to walk away and keep looking for the best breeder in the trade of these parrots.

- Make sure to ask the right questions like how and when they were weaned, the food the hatchlings were fed, etc. And be ready to answer a few of the breeders own when you get the ball of purchasing rolling. Any good breeder would show interest about where their temporary wards are going.

- A young Pionus is not to be given to anyone before the 12-14 week mark or the period when they have naturally weaned from their mothers. Doing so any earlier would most likely equate to big trouble. Young Pionus parrots taken home at this time may be fed with foods that it has been given whilst with the breeder. As it grows you will want to slowly mix in with its usual diet and introduce other beneficial foods, supplemented with vitamins (if recommended by vet), like vegetables and fruits.

- Be sure that you are given an opportunity to visit the avian facilities to see the living conditions of the birds yourself. By this time you would have empowered yourself with important facts to be able to spot a healthy bird from an unhealthy one. You would have read and found out what to expect at certain pet establishments whether commercial or private and would be able to tell a shoddy setting from a legitimate one.

- While most if not all have the potential to be taught to speak, it has been reported and fact-proven that the Maximilian, along with the Blue-headed Pionus are the most likely to pick up words quicker and with ease than the other Pionus sorts. The Maxilian is also quite the mild-mannered one not adverse to loud hoot calls or loud discordant noises. You might want to check if the bird has been taught to speak by the breeder.

- You can also find great avian breeders online but you have to take into consideration the validity of the breeder. It is highly recommended that you see your new bird in person before buying anything on the internet. You can find several recommended list of

How to Spot a Healthy Pionus

- Observe the bird in its habitat and check for anomalies that belie a healthy bird. A healthy bird should be sprite, active, perky, lively, mobile, can stand on two feet, and both eyes and ears clear and alert.

- Observe its appetite and drinking habits. Does it eagerly eat its food and drink water? Study its feathers and look for the presence of balding or bald spots. Its feathers should lay close to the body, not out of place, ruffled or continuously fluffed.

- Both feet and legs of the bird must be free of bumps or lumps, should be smooth and there should be no signs of rough scales or scabs.

- If possible, spend as much time as you can with your prospective new Pionus birds before buying it. Interact with the bird and see how it is with you.

- Continue the diet of the bird as advised by the store owner or breeder to maintain its eating habits. Look for any health problems or issues as well.

  •Only purchase a parrot that is banded. Banding means the bird have a small metal band on one of its legs placed at birth by the breeder which is inscribed with the bird's clutch number, date of birth and the breeder number. Leg bands are indicators that the purchaser and the bird itself are in the country legally and have not been smuggled.

Chapter Five: Nutrition and Feeding

The pionus parrot is surprisingly robust and is easy to care for. As with any responsibility a new or existing pet owner takes on, taking care of a pionus is no different. Making sure that we are ready and aware of the undertakings of raising a pet is the needful mindset when going into a commitment of raising any animal.

We will be looking into what it takes, with regard to the feeding, nutrition, grooming as well as housing enclosure needs of the pionus parrots. You will discover that it is not at all difficult to care for one or two as long as you ready yourself for the demands of your new pet. Since the pionus takes just a wee amount of time to get acclimated to its new surroundings you will find that most of the adjusting will come from your end - that is when you decide to commit to raise a pionus parrot and welcome it home.

Start off your new relationship with trust and build on that as you provide for the needs of a pionus according to what it requires to thrive under your care. The pionus has been known to enjoy a lengthy lifespan so it is a matter not to be taken lightly. You will soon understand that a relationship as such will enrich your life if you are prepared.

Caring for and Feeding Your Pionus

In their natural habitat the Pionus birds ingest seeds, fruits, berries, and blossoms are likely to be in their diet as well. Most Pionus birds are also fond of eating corns that comes from well – cultivated corn fields. A healthy Pionus diet consisting of a well - formulated bird foods, a range of seeds, and a good helping of dried fruits is usually thought of as a suitable food base because it provides a nutritious variety of parrot mix. Alongside these base foods, you should aim to feed your pet with a supplement of vegetables and fresh fruits.

The Pionus parrot is a naturally active bird and could become overweight when in confinement just like their relatives - the Amazon parrots, which is why a low – fat type of diet is much suitable for these creatures. Proper care for any pet, notwithstanding the Pionus, starts with giving the bird a good diet especially sprouting seed which contain high amino acids and is low in fat, are food sources good for their health. Of course, your avian vet will be a crucial player in this area. Networking with other pionus parrot owners will also be a wise investment of time and will give you greater insight on the experiences of those who have started caring for these small parrots.

Bird Food

Available foods for Pionus birds include formulated type of diets like extruded or pelleted parrot mixes or a pure seed mix which could be both beneficial. There are upsides and downsides to feeding your pet with either a mix diet or a seed – only diet as you will need to give your parrots supplemental vitamins and minerals. You would also need to measure out these supplements properly.

Be sure to give your birds fresh, natural foods in the form of vegetables and fruits. Cut it up into tiny bits and mix just the proper ratio of any of the above mixtures with the fresh. Water is to be provided fresh frequently throughout the day so make sure there will be someone who can replace water in their water dishes.

Formulated Diet

A diet of formulated foods can give your pet with a proper nutritional base so that you won't have to add or buy other ingredients. On the other hand formulated food alone does not have the phytonutrients or the antioxidant pigments which can be found in grains, seeds, vegetables, and fruits. Phytonutrients are thought to help strengthen the bird's immune system, aid the body to self-heal, and is said to prevent common illnesses. Another con is that parrots can also get bored with just a diet that lacks variety such as those found in formulated feeds.

Seed Diet

Giving your pionus this type of diet offers them a lot more variety in terms of food mixes but will require additional calcium and vitamins. Food variation should be your most important concern because it is vital in the diet of a pionus especially for its psychological enrichment, so do not forget to be inventive about the variety of fresh foods you mix in with commercial bird food mixes.

Supplements and Water

Supplemental food you can put into the formulated or seed diet mix would be different kinds of fruits such as plums, cherries, apples, pears, bananas, mangos, grapes, oranges, papayas, blueberries, and strawberries.

All sorts of sprouted seeds and vegetables also make good alternatives such as zucchini, carrots, cucumbers, and a lot of other garden vegetables including chickweed and dandelions. You should also feed them food that is rich in calcium and Vitamin A improves vision and can also boost immunity. Eggs and meat are good sources of Vitamin A as well as different types of vegetables like carrots, kale broccoli, sweet potatoes, cantaloupe and squash. Too much or not enough of Vitamin A can potentially leave your parrots vulnerable to diseases. Since Pionus birds have different species, it is best to consult with your avian veterinarian first to know the right amount of Vitamin A your pet needs.

Pionus parrot also need high levels of protein or amino acids to build their tissues, feathers, muscles and skin. Birds in general can produce their own amino acids. However, there are some amino acids such as threonine, tryptophan, lysine, methionine, phenylalanine and that some birds are not able to produce or sustain in its body. The sources of these essential amino acids are available in today's bird diet products. Calcium on the other hand is needed to make bones grow stronger and it also allows calcification of eggshells in birds. In captivity, you can provide calcium in the form of a cuttlebone or calcium treat that is attached inside your bird cage. You can also offer a powdered supplement such as packaged oyster shell which can be added directly to your pet's food. Follow the instructions on the supplement package. Calcium is also vital for muscle contraction, blood clotting and heart functions.

In terms of hydration, water is just as important for birds as it is for human beings especially during hot weather conditions to avoid dehydration. Parrots may drink ten times its normal water intake during summer which is why they should be given access to clean, fresh and cool water. Do not use tap water because can cause the bird to be ill, as well as distilled water, instead use unflavored bottled drinking water or bottled natural spring water. If in case, tap water is used, treat it with a de-chlorinating treatment. Inability to provide fresh water to pet birds can cause upset stomach with unbearable stomachache. Water is vital to maintain cells, digestion, feathers, and metabolism. All water given to birds for drinking, as well as water used for misting, soaking or bathing must be 100% free of chlorine and heavy metals.

Keep in mind that your pionus parrots, whether hand raised or otherwise, have a set of staple foods that it would need in order to stay healthy. In their natural habitat they would have to forage for food. In your loving care, those abilities to hunt and "bring home the bacon" is mostly left up to you for provision. Make sure that you are providing it the most optimum of foods as it doesn't take too much to do this. You will find that some of the foods it will need are already available in your fruit and vegetable basket. Veggies/fruits you want to avoid feeding your pionus parrot is avocados as this can potentially be toxic to most birds. Toxic food also includes onions, alcohol, mushrooms, tomato leaves, caffeine, dried beans, parsley, chocolate, and junk food.

Chapter Six: Housing, Bird Rooms and Maintenance

Pionus parrots can quickly adjust to their surroundings or aviary, therefore it won't take much on your end to keep it happy and healthy as long as you provide it a dwelling place suitable to its needs to give it a leg up and allow it to thrive well. Most Pionus parrots are usually kept in an aviary inside the owner's house. Cages should never be confining and must have enough space for subtle flight, so buy one where your pet will be comfortable in. This chapter will give you caging measurements and tips on how to maintain a good environment for your pet.

Cage Measurements for Pionus Parrots

Sometimes, if there is ample space in the home or alternatively in an aviary. Remember that it will be important to bird-proof your home and to figure out early on how you intend to raise the birds and where in the home you will house them. If it were one or two in a big house, it would be easy to make deductions and adjustments. Should you choose more than a pair to keep as pets and raise, consider not only space, but factor time away from what you normally do in your life. It will take an equal portion of patience, time, dedication and commitment to clean out and maintain cages and individual parrots.

Get a cage with dimensions similar to the aviary size of an Amazon parrot. It can be between 100 - 150 centimeters (39 in – 59 in) high and have a floor space of 60 x 100 centimeters (23 in x 39 in). 3/4" bar spacing is recommended, but you can choose to have a 1 inch bar spacing for the larger pionus species.

The aviary that you should provide should have a room with which your bird can feel free but still have a space for perches, bowls other cage requirements. Toys can include ropes, chains, bells, bird swings and wooden or other bird toys. A playpen is also recommended so that your bird can have more space to roam around.

Pionus parrots in general can do quite well in an outdoor aviary especially when they are already acclimated to that kind of environment. However not all of them can stand cold temperatures. For instance the Bronze-winged Pionus must not be housed where temperatures fall under 41°F (5°C), and the Dusky Pionus should not be housed in temperatures below 50 ° F (10° C).

When housing a pionus in an outdoor cage, the aviary has to have a shelter that is protected and can be cooled and heated in areas that are necessary. It may also be ideal to have a flight cage attached in it. A recommended measurement of the cage is around 180 - 240 centimeters long. For exercise, play and to stave boredom attach a perch at each end.

For a couple of birds the ideal base width could measure about 90 - 120 cm for two parrots. Keep in mind that you should also take the time to maintain a clean cage because the continued good health of your parrot depends on it. Most pathogens, viruses, diseases, bacteria and fungi stem from an unkempt enclosure and this will definitely pave the way for illness to fall upon your sweet birds.

Make sure that you outfit the aviary with necessary sundries that would allow your active but fairly quiet birds opportunities to play, exercise and practice their innate skills. Maintaining the cage includes daily replenishment of your pet's water and food in dishes. Make it a weekly habit to wash all of the perches and playing materials of your parrots.

The base of the cage has to be washed out at least once or twice a week. You should thoroughly hose the aviary and disinfect it at least twice a year. You should also replace things like old dishes, toys and perches at least once a year. Keep a shallow dish of cool water made available to the parrots for bathing and drinking. Mostly all these parrots enjoy bathing and there are a number of reasons to provide them with daily bathing opportunities which is good both for their health and well-being. Add a few drops of hydrogen peroxide or GSE in its bathing water to help prevent infections. GSE has excellent anti-parasitic properties and gives an additional benefit to the bath and health of the parrots.

The following recommended cage dimensions are 4 feet wide by 4 feet tall by 6 to 8 feet long. Facilitate sanitation by use of suspended cages. Suspended cages ensure droppings and food remnants fall through the wire floor of the cage. Nest boxes of a grandfather-style work best. A well suited size is 10" wide x 10" deep x 18-24" high. Ideally, the nest box should be placed high up in a dark, secluded area of the aviary.

Bird Proofing Rooms

Once your bird get comfortable enough around its enclosure you will want to give it some outside time and allow it to inspect other areas of the bird room, or possibly your home. You will need to take stock and keep a number of things in check in order to keep the bird safe whilst outside its cage. You will have to make sure that there are no escape areas where the bird could fly out and get lost forever. Take the proper measures to ensure the safe flight and wandering of your pionus within your home. You will have to remove household hazards that would pose threat and danger to your pionus parrot. Safety is very important because birds are much more sensitive to a few chemicals than people are.

Keep in mind that birds use their beaks and mouths to explore, and they will likely want to taste anything at least once - that is all it would take for it to get into deep trouble should it come across a really deadly chemical. Many household hazards could cause your bird injury or to some degree be dangerous to the bird when eaten, inhaled, or if they come in contact with your parrot. While some may cause only mild reactions some chemicals can cause instant death, so it is best to remove them from areas where your bird could get into contact with these.

- Avoid placing its cage in areas where it is too hot or too cold or drafty. For obvious reasons, you will not want to allow your bird anywhere a ceiling or a standard fan. Keep its cage away from fans and do not keep fans in the room where they are housed. If unavoidable, remember to switch off all fans before you allow the bird out of its cage. For extra measure you might want to put a clamped cover which you can lock over the fan switch to avoid accidentally switching it on. Aside from the keeping your parrots away from fans, you want to make sure that all your windows are shut and covered.

- Glass panes may not be immediately visible to the birds and may cause it to slam into one unknowingly. Like birds in the wild, glass panes are foreign to your pionus parrots. A precaution you could take is clipping the bird's wings. Although it won't prevent the bird from taking flight, clipping would slow it down. Consider a flight suit with a lanyard which would limit its span of flight. Cover all windows so that it does not see the outside from its vantage. Keep your bird's nails trimmed as snagging itself on drapes and curtains is a great possibility.

- Check that all screens are installed and fastened securely and make sure that you regularly check them for holes and ripped areas where wire sticks out and could injure your birds.

- Birds like to find small nooks and corners to hide in and where they can nest. Being as small as they are and quiet as they may sometime be, it would be difficult to locate a lost bird even in a small house. Limit its area of movement and keep them out of cluttered room, rooms where there are wires, electronics like computers, printers, washers, dryer's mechanical devices and breakables. Make sure that you check cupboards and cabinets before closing them lest the bird had managed to get in the space. Look where you walk as small inquisitive birds will be easy targets to hurried feet.

- Make sure that your birds are inside their enclosures when laying new sheets on the beds, when you throw in laundry in the washer because a bird could walk into a layer of sheets unnoticed.

- Air ducts where the bird could crawl into and get lost in should be covered.

- Birds are crazy over string and anything that mimics string will not be spared from the inquisitive and curious pionus. Keep all cords and live wires covered with plastic spiral wraps. It will not stop the bird from investigating them, but it will give you a sense of ease knowing that it will not accidentally electrocute itself on a live wire or destroy any of your electronic gadgets.

- Pionus birds are good pets for families with children because they are friendly and easily warm up to people once acclimated. But never leave a child and a bird unsupervised and make sure that you teach a young child how to handle a bird under watchful supervision.

- If you have established pets of the four legged sort as cats or dogs, be mindful to apply the same rule as you would with children and never leave them alone unattended. If you have fish in an aquarium, make sure that the aquarium is covered to avoid accidental drowning of your bird or unintended ingestion of you fish by your bird. So goes for reptile cages. It is best to keep them away from each other and raise them in different areas of the house. Not only are heating lamps and the cords that power surges through pose danger to the bird, the reptile itself may be a predator of your pet bird.

- Your kitchen is virtually a death trap for your little pionus flyer. Fumes from pans, ovens, chemical solutions are mostly very toxic to the small avian. Keep them out of the kitchen when on a cooking spree. Open pots of boiling water could also become an invitation for disaster if a bird in flight mistakes it for a bath. Margarine, butter and lard could mat the feathers of the bird making it difficult for the parrot to move.

- Caffeinated beverages, avocados, salt, coffee grounds, coffee beans and the like as well as all kinds of chocolate are highly toxic to birds including your pionus parrot. Tea, cola, garlic, salt, onion, yeast dough are other toxic foods that you want to keep away from your pionus parrots.

- Keep the doors of your baths and toilets closed as these places have fumes and water reservoirs which could cause accidental inhalation or drowning of the bird.

- Any sort of heat source is a danger to your bird. Keep them away from heaters, open flames, hot pots and pans, hot irons - whether for clothing or hair as these emit fumes dangerous to your pionus parrots.

- Do not allow your bird out of its cage on dinner nights when candles are in order. Pen flames whether from an oven, or a candle could at the very least singe your bird and at worst make it a distressed flying ball of feathers.

- Dangerous chemicals around the home are aplenty what with regular and routine cleaning sprees; we use chemical solutions on almost anything we need to tidy.

- Arsenic, zinc and lead are very toxic to people and more so to birds. There are a lot of dangerous metals around our houses which pose grave threats to your pionus parrots. Make sure that the cage you buy for your parrots are free of these metals. To be sure, avoid buying cages from garage sales and second-hand bins from flea markets.

- Herbicides like slug and snail bait, anti-tick and anti-flea insecticides, pesticides like roach, mosquito, ant and rat poison are other dangerous poisons has to be kept out of sight and never used around your pionus bird.

- Tinsel around the tree and Christmas decorations are other hazards that could entrap or snag your bird accidentally. Trees in the wild are not decorated or dressed with garlands but the bird is not any wiser. You may want to limit outside time or switch play time releases to another room of the house during this time of the year.

Chapter Seven: Temperament and Training

Like most parrots the pionus needs a bit of time to become accustomed to its new environment and when allowed this time of adjustment, a hand raised Pionus will definitely delight you with its company. Your pionus may, at first, seem a little standoffish when you initially bring it home, but staying quiet and reserved is a natural reaction until it has checked out its new surroundings until it feels secure. Once over that hurdle - which shouldn't take more than a couple of weeks you will see that it is a good companion and pet. This chapter will give you some tips on how to handle, train and socialize them.

Social Behaviors

In their natural habitats, when these birds are not breeding, Pionus parrots appear in small or medium flocks of around 10 to 60 birds. When breeding season comes around, pionus parrots are generally seen either alone or in pairs. When in captivity Pionus parrots are not particularly loud and generally peaceful. A sweet Pionus behavior is that they are typically calm birds save for a few individuals who can be a bit more skittish. This nervous behavior is only apparent upon introduction to a new environment.

This soon passes once they become more confident about their surroundings. It has been observed and reported that female pionus parrots are more gentle their male counterparts. These parrots are utterly social birds and are frequently thought to be the most ideal parrot to keep as a pet, specifically when children are involved. They are steadfastly loyal and have good, calm personalities. A favorite trait of the Pionus is that they rarely ever bite, hence the popularity with children. They also do quite well with other established pets if given the proper amount of time get used to and accept each other. But be very mindful to supervise all groupings especially with larger animals and with tiny children to avoid any unexpected accidents.

Training and Handling Pionus Parrots

Although a Pionus parrot has been known to adapt quickly to its new home, you still have to give the new arrival a couple of days or a bit more to get use to you, your voice and its new cage before you attempt to handle it. A hand fed baby will not need much taming since it would be used to human attention and often can be handled right away. First of all, in order to be able to train and handle your parrot will depend on it trusting you, so be consistent, go slowly and be more patient. A lot of parrots are usually the most receptive to training during the evening. It is best if each session is limited to below 20 minutes taking hour long breaks to rest in between.

Keep in mind that bird training and bird taming takes patience so toss that iron glove out because this will not work at all. When punishment is meted this would only serve to destroy the trust you are working on to build.

Initial Training

Your initial aim would be to get the parrot to gain your trust and accept a treat you offer it. This will lead to the parrot to let you to tenderly scratch its head. You can then begin to work on getting the bird to step up on your hand. This would depend on how tame the bird is. These first two goals could be instantaneous like with a hand fed baby pionus or it might take several weeks or more for an untamed bird. Pionus parrots are not the cuddly sort of bird, however they do like it when their head, neck and ears is scratched.

Advanced Training

As soon as your pionus parrot gets over its shyness, you can both begin working on training it for speech. The keys to get your Pionus parrot talking would be frequency and repetition. Almost all parrots can learn at least a few select words, but compared to the African Grey, their mimicry sounds rather raspy and 'parrot-like.'

Try looking for a complete course in training parrots because it could turn your bird into a fun, and a more loving companion. It will also get to learn a lot of cool tricks. At any rate make sure to factor in time for you and your bird to socialize. Your reward doing so is getting to know the individuality of your birds, including strengths and weaknesses.

Playtime Activities

Play and exercise are activities important for the psychological health and physical well-being of your Pionus. They are active by nature so be sure to provide your pionus with a lot of exercise equipment fit for them. Otherwise they may become overweight and if they do they will become sedentary birds.

Activities also help prevent problems and deter stress like screeching. Give your parrot lots of fun activities to keep it occupied, such as bird ladders, ropes, chains (preferably large), parrot swings, fresh branches to gnaw and chew, and remember to switch it up with new bird toys on a regular basis.

Chapter Eight: Grooming Needs and Health Care

Keeping your pionus happy and healthy would mean that you will have to take time to pay them mind and attention with regard to body maintenance and grooming. Not only does grooming your pionus avoid it from getting sick, routine grooming also minimizes the chances of it getting snagged, accidentally clipped or hurt. This chapter will provide you information on how to groom your pet parrots as well as the list of common bird diseases that can affect their health.

Importance of Grooming Your Parrot

Pionus parrots love a good rain shower and have been observed to languish under a mild shower in its natural habitat. You will want to raise your pionus parrot and have it thrive in captivity whilst attempting to mimic its natural environment as closely as possible. You will need to be inventive about some things like providing a shower bath for it.

Once again, looking up other pionus owners in your local or online will give you the advantage of finding out what worked for other owners and suggestions they may have. Of course, as with humans, pionus parrots despite general qualities and traits they may share are still individuals with their own set of behavior and habits. Take this time to observe and get to know your parrots better and you will be happy to discover their individualities.

Bird Baths

Shower is very good to maintain skin and plumage conditions. It is a crucial part of the personal hygiene of your Pionus parrot. Pionus enjoy the rain dearly and would even lie on its back as it spreads and flap their wings as a sign of utmost enjoyment.

A good way to replicate a natural rain shower is by using either a good spray head or a hand held shower sprayer. Set the temperature to lukewarm and let it run in an indoor shower or in an aviary.

Wings

Right off the bat, you don't want to clip a baby parrots wings as it will need time to learn how to use them; first is to trim the wings of the parrot, you should do it in a regular basis especially if you prefer in discouraging it from taking flight. Make sure that you do this routinely to prevent your pet flying out and losing it. On the downside clipping their wings too much could result in them crash landing or the inability to take proper flight resulting in injury. You also need to know that if you intend on showing your Pionus Parrot the wings are not to be clipped. Allowing your bird to fly around the house can knock over things, get the bird into unwanted situations, lose its feathers in accidents or even injure itself. On the other hand why keep a bird around if it can't do what it is supposed to do and fly? There are many conflicting opinions about whether to clip or not to clip a parrot's wings. Consider this fact and answer that question. Consulting with few experienced parrot keepers wouldn't hurt either.

Don't forget to ask your bird trainer and vet for any recommendations they may have about this matter. Be ready to answer some questions as well. It is very imperative that you watch and learn for the first few clippings of its wings and employ the services of a professional before attempting to do it on your own.

Consider using a clicker to train the bird to return to you for periods when it is given outside time to take supervised flights. Another advantage of a clicker is how it helps avert "bad" behavior from your parrot. The obvious person to assist you on learning to train your bird is your parrot trainer. Take time to sit in during sessions as this is as much for you as it is for the pionus.

Beak

There are precautions to take with regard to the beak care of your parrot. If the beak becomes overgrown or deformed it then needs to be trimmed. However it is usual for the upper beak of this parrot to be a tad longer compared to that of other parrots.

There are a lot of items to help your bird keep its beak in shape and can be found and bought at local pet stores like lava blocks, mineral blocks, and other beak grooming items where they can file their beaks down on their own. However much like its feet, the pionus parrot has a small quick at the end of its beak which you can file down using an emery board. Be careful that you don't file too much or you may injure the bird. Keep in mind that you will want to sit in and learn the techniques of how to carry out the procedure before doing it yourself.

Nails

The nails of your parrot serve their purpose for the bird. However, If the nails of your pionus becomes too long this may prevent your bird from perching properly. Overgrown nails could also cause it to unintentionally scratch you. Be aware of the birds quick though as cutting too far into the nail will result to injuring the quick and cause bleeding. Always have styptic compound handy and a ball of cotton. Keep in mind that the quick grows along with the nail and over calculating on a long nail and cutting to deeply will hurt the bird.

The nails of the pionus should be trimmed if they become overgrown for its safety and yours. Fortunately there is a vast assortment of concrete sort perches which are available at pet shops that would help keep the nails of the parrot trimmed. You want to invest on a good pair of clippers. You can find them online and at pet shops along with, a good product to have handy, styptic powder which helps to stop bleeding in the event of over-cutting the bird's nails.

Health Care

In this section, you will learn about the diseases that may affect and threaten your parrot's wellness. Learning these diseases as well as its remedies is vital for you and your bird so that you could prevent it from happening or even help with its treatment in case they caught one. Below are some of the most common health problems that occur specifically to Pionus parrots. You will learn some guidelines on how these diseases can be prevented and treated as well as its signs and symptoms.

Bacterial/Parasitic Infections

Bacterial infections usually occur during the breeding process of parrots. Bacteria and Parasites usually target the intestines and digestive tract of the birds, which then causes diarrhea. If you think that your bird's feces are sticky rather than loose, it's a sign that your bird might be infected. As a precaution, you should bring him/her to a veterinarian for a lab report to prevent the infection

The treatment for birds infected consists of several anti-parasitic medicines that are fortunately available to the vet, after which, your vet will suggest you to make your bird undergo lab tests to monitor and ensure that the medicine killed the virus.

Bird Pox

Bird pox is caused by an poxvirus infection and it causes real damage to Pionus parrots and scarred them for life. The virus is usually transmitted through a direct contact with birds carrying the virus. Biting insects or any contaminated surfaces may spread the disease even further and may make the pain worse. The thickening of the eyes by mucous membranes is a sign that your parrot is a carrier of the virus. It manifests through a wet form of the pox that affects, mouth, gullet, and upper and lower respiratory systems. Veterinarians typically recommend 10,000 units of Vitamin A which are given by injection. Antibiotics are also given to treat secondary infections and a Mercurochrome solution is given to treat their mucous-thickened eyes. Consult an avian veterinarian immediately.

E – Coli

Another common illness that affects parrots is a bacterium called E-Coli. It is very rampant among psittacine birds. E-Coli is a gram-negative bacteria found in guts of birds that are considered abnormal; this bacteria is highly capable of causing diseases especially if it reaches into the bird's bloodstream, respiratory system, and reproductive system or if the carrier parrot is under a stressful situation.

Coliform infections are the main cause of deaths in most parrots, the E-Coli bacteria weakens the bird's digestive and respiratory system most of the time. A sudden loss appetite and difficulty in breathing may be a sign that your bird is suffering from this bacteria. Veterinarians usually have to determine first if these bacteria are the disease causing agents or merely a secondary infection through a culture testing before treating it with antibiotics or other necessary medicines.

Wasting Disease

This disease is commonly known as Wasting Disease, is an inflammatory wasting disease caused by a virus called Avian BornaVirus (ABV), which is mostly found in Psittacine species like Pionus parrots. It primarily affects the Central Nervous System and multiple organs such as liver, kidneys, heart, brain, peripheral blood vessels, lungs and gastrointestinal tract.

It is classified as a sporadic disease that has a very rare kind of attack to a bird's immune system. Unlike other virus which attacks the whole cell then move to another cell, ABV does not destroy the cells which leave the infected ones very little damage. Since the cells are not destroyed the immune system cannot detect it and thus the virus stays within the bird for an indefinite amount of time, which eventually weakens the immune system and results in continuous infections throughout the parrot's life. Avian veterinarians have difficulties in detecting the virus because of other infections it can bring to the bird's health. The ABV does not show-up in the test results and there are other viruses similar to ABV which may also lead in the assumption that the bird is not a carrier even if it is.

ABV is also an asymptomatic virus, which means that there are no signs that the bird might be infected or a carrier. However, sometimes you can notice it if your pet experienced instances of mild disorders such as moaning, feather-plucking or self-mutilation to severe illness such as head tremors, paralysis, seizures or other sudden sickness due to infected organs in the body. Veterinarians classified the severity of disease and level of impact to different stages such as low-to-moderate symptoms to severe and chronic stages.

Parrots in the early stages are given treatment to prevent the virus from spreading and eventually curing it. Although, this virus can be controlled and has a remedy, it's important that your bird always goes for checkup and undergo medical tests every now and then especially if it was diagnosed with the virus before.

Coacal Papilloma

It is caused by a virus infection similar to warts in other animals and it is transmitted through direct contact. These tiny tumors usually appear in the vent area of a parrot where it can eventually block the fecal area of making it hard for the bird to defecate if it grows large enough. The recommended treatment for this is a laser surgery. As a remedy veterinarians also advised owners to offer Jalapeño peppers to prevent and control papilloma in birds. Consult your avian vet on the right amount of peppers to feed to your Pionus.

Parrot Fever

It is a zoonotic infectious disease caused by an unknown organism whose natural hosts are birds such as Pionus birds. It is an airborne disease and it can also be spread via the bird's feces. This disease is highly contagious.

Before acquiring a parrot, it's important that your bird goes through a Psittacosis test because this type of infection can also potentially harm a human being. The worst thing about this disease is that it is asymptomatic, which means symptoms does not appear or cannot be detected easily, you will never know when it could happen and if the bird is a carrier. This type of disease is asymptomatic that sometimes even a psittacosis test could not detect the disease. Identifying organisms in the feces is done in most cases.

This disease is treated with a tetracycline based antibiotic given for about 45 days to eliminate the carrier state, although some veterinarians believe that the antibiotic does not necessarily remove the carrier state.

Pacheco's Disease

This disease is caused by a herpes virus which attacks the liver and results in acute liver failure. It is very contagious and highly fatal to most birds. Diagnosis is done via necropsy which detects microscopic evidences of the virus found in the liver.

Unfortunately, there is no guaranteed antibiotic or remedy for this disease, the best you could do is to minimize the spread of the virus through intensive care and some antiviral medication.

Aspergillosis

It is a respiratory disease caused by the fungus called *Aspergillus*, which is found in warm and moist environments. The microscopic spores of Aspergillus are an airborne transmitted disease. The fungus does not cause the disease per se but if your bird does not have a healthy immune system it can cause illness. It increases the chances of the spores being inhaled by your bird if the environment has poor ventilation and sanitation, dusty conditions, and in close confinements.

Other predisposing factors include poor nutrition, other medical conditions in the respiratory system and prolonged use of antibiotics or corticosteroids, which eventually weakens the immune system. Aspergillosis is more common in parrots than other pet birds. There are two kinds of Aspergillosis, it's either acute or chronic, both of which attacks the respiratory system. Acute Aspergillosis signs and symptoms include symptoms like severe difficulty in breathing, cyanosis (a bluish coloration of mucous membranes and/or skin), decreased or loss of appetite, frequent drinking and urination. In chronic Aspergillosis symptoms include white nodules that appear through the respiratory tissue, large numbers of spores enter the bloodstream, infection in the kidneys, skin, muscle, gastrointestinal tract, liver, eyes, and brain.

Aspergillosis is generally difficult to detect until complete diagnosis. Do not compromise respiratory infections, consult the veterinarian immediately.

Always consult a veterinarian first to know the right remedy for your bird. There are reports that the antifungal drug Itraconazole may also be toxic to some Pionus parrots than to other bird species. Another antifungal drug called Amphotericin B may be administered orally, topically, by injection, or nebulizing. Consult your vet for proper guidance. Surgery may also be performed to remove accessible lesions. Supportive care is often needed such as oxygen, supplemental heat, tube feeding, and treatment of underlying conditions.

Maintaining a good husbandry and diet can highly prevent outbreaks of Aspergillosis.

Psittacine Beak and Feather Disease (PBFD)

PBFD is a viral condition that is responsible for damage to the beak, feathers and nails as well as the immune system of infected birds. These are very common in parrots between 6 months and 3 years of age. PBFD typically affects the feathers of infected birds as well as its beak and nails over time.

Some signs and symptoms that your pet might have PBFD includes feathers are short, fragile, malformed, and prone to bleeding and breaking. Birds may first lose their the white, fine powder produced by specialized feathers to help maintain feather health when this happens more abnormal feathers will eventually develop. The beak may also become glossy rather than the more typical matte appearance, nails and beak becomes brittle and malformed, significant loss of feathers (as the follicles become damaged), loss of appetite and regurgitation or continuous vomiting.

Veterinarians will likely perform a PCR test to confirm the diagnosis. This test uses advanced techniques to look for the virus' DNA. Most of the time PCR only needs a blood sample, but your veterinarian may also need to take a swab from your bird's mouth and vent.

The majority of clinically affected birds will die within a few months to a year because there are no antiviral drugs available to fight the virus. Your avian veterinarian can only help keep your bird comfortable because this condition is painful for the bird and it also allows secondary infections to take hold. Some birds may survive for a few months they will ultimately die from this disease.

The only thing breeders and pet owners can do to prevent this deadly virus is to take pro-active steps but since you can't help the birds mingle with other birds as they travel from wholesaler to retail pet distributors to your home the best solution is to have your bird examined by an avian veterinarian and allow diagnostic testing. It is also wise to take your bird for a yearly exam to make sure it stays healthy. Yearly exams can catch small issues before they get worse.

Tracheal Mites

Tracheal Mites are quite common in birds because it can infiltrate the bird's entire respiratory tract and the severity of the infection can vary greatly. Birds with mild infections may not show any signs but severe infections may produce symptoms including trouble breathing, wheezing or clicking sounds, open-mouth breathing, and excessive salivation. This disease can be transmitted through close contact with an infected bird and through airborne particles. It can also be passed through contaminated food or drinking water. It is quite difficult to diagnose if your parrots has tracheal mites, veterinarians often recommend performing a tracheal swab to check under a microscope for further evaluation.

Common signs include sneezing, wheezing or difficulty in breathing. Continuous bobbing of the tail while breathing is also a sign that your Pionus may have a respiratory problem. Tracheal mites also overlap with a number of other infections that has the same symptoms, so you need to make sure you have an accurate diagnosis.

Medications are available to treat the disease, though dosage can be tricky and many birds die from tracheal mites. It is best to consult your veterinarian first before getting any treatment options available for tracheal mites.

Chapter Nine: Breeding Your Pionus Parrots

If you decide to start breeding Pionus birds you will want to seek the help of an expert and work with them closely. The whole point of breeding is to improve the specie population and give it a good chance of living a healthy life. This chapter will give you some basic information and guidelines on how to determine your bird's sex as well as the proper was on how to breed them and also information regarding their reproduction.

Pionus Parrot Sexing

Sexing parrots can be very tricky for a novice and should not be attempted by any one inexperienced in determining and identifying bird gender. DNA has been the one of the more popular ways to determine the gender of birds because it is non-invasive, quick and safe.

Other times, especially if the bird is intended to be used for breeding purposes, an endoscopy is suggested by vets as this not shows the sex of the bird, the procedure also allows avian vets to check internally for any inconsistencies that would hinder breeding. The color of the Pionus parrot is not a visual indication of the bird's gender. So make sure you have to sexing pairs before you attempt to breed them - putting two male parrots in one cage would be an invitation for disaster.

Breeding/Reproduction

If you do decide to breed your Pionus parrots you have to be ready for the work and responsibility as well as time consuming efforts to not only make sure you are providing it with its proper needs but also overseeing and handling maintenance duties to keep your birds contented, thriving and happy. Make sure to check with local authorities in your country and locale to find out if there are regulations to follow. There are currently no legal guidelines to this in the UK, America or Canada.

Breeding Environment

Cages and enclosures you make, buy or build should ideally have enough if not ample space for your birds to enjoy flying. Remember that it is in the bird's nature to fly around and if not given the space it needs, it may develop behavioral problems that would be difficult to deal.

Make sure your bird's enclosure is spacious enough and fitted properly with the correct equipment to promote exercise and physical activities. Make sure that its enclosure is furnished with sundries that would not only allow it physical exercise but mental stimulation as well. Keep in mind that the Pionus parrot is one smart polly and will need to stay sharp to maintain good mental health. Setting up a conducive enclosure for your birds will also come in handy if and when you decide to breed them.

Egg Laying and Hatchlings

A female Pionus parrot could lay up to 5 eggs and will brood for around 26 days after producing the eggs.

Depending on the species the young Pionus will get ready to leave the nest anywhere between the period of 8 - 14 weeks of age.

Perhaps not as vibrantly colored like some other parrots, the smaller Pionus parrot develop into their shimmering feather colors as they grow up and mature. Younger Pionus birds will display a more muted version of their adult colors which will later become more apparent as time goes by. With their squarish stubby tails, and distinctive red undertail feather markings, the Pionus develops into quite a stunning bird in its own right.

Most of the Pionus parrots share the same predominantly green-colored bodies but each one has their own distinct colors identifying their sort.

Potential Health Problems

As advised by vets all over to pet owners of all sorts of animals providing the best bird health care begins with a clean enclosure. Medical problems will be greatly avoided if you provide them a good environment.

Get to know your pet bird in order for you to be able to spot any indications of illness. A sick parrot must be taken to a veterinarian knowledgeable on avian health care for diagnosis and treatment. Like all other parrots, signs of sickness you need to be aware of sometimes obvious.

Good bird health is shown apparent when the parrot is active, mobile, able to do the usual things it would like hop, jump, take steps, fly, eat, drink, bathe and interact.

Plumage out of place is a sign of illness and should not be taken lightly. If you notice a lack of interest in physical activities, a bird sleeping or resting at the floor base of its cage, or puffiness, consider these other indications of possible illness in the parrot and would deem an immediate visit to the vet. Discharge and crusting seen at the underside, around the vent or undertail area of a Pionus could indicate illness as with feet that look weak. Lack of appetite is another sign of your bird feeling under the weather and you should investigate what is causing this. Cloudy peepers, any sort of discharge from eyes or nose, diarrhea, and sneezing are other indicative signs of a sick bird. Be sure that you have a good reliable, experienced and successful avian vet to run to in case of emergencies and more importantly, regular medical checkups and possibly testing.

Life Span and Availability

These robust wee parrots are a hardy bunch often living for as long as 25 years with some noted to exist beyond those years!

Five out of the eight species of Pionus parrots are often available as captive raised pets in the United States. The Pionus birds consistently up for sale include the Bronze-winged Pionus, the Blue-headed Pionus, the Maximilian's Pionus or Scaly-headed Parrot, the White-capped Parrot or White-crowned Pionus and the Dusky Pionus.

Due to recent captive breeding becoming more successful, the Pionus species have become more readily available in the pet bird trade. The three remaining species of Pionus are quite rare and not commonly available for sale presently. The rare or unavailable Pionus in the market are the plum-crowned Pionus or Restless Parrot Pionus tumultuosus a.k.a. the Plum-crowned Parrot, the Pionus sordidus also known as the Red-billed Parrot/Coral-billed Pionus or Sordid Pionus and the White-headed Pionus also known as the Massena's Parrot or the White-headed Parrot Pionus seniloides.

Of the all Pionus species in the wild some of them have been made available to the pet trade in the US but others are hard to find in this country. Some of them more frequently accessible than others are the blue-headed Pionus along with the scaly-headed, bronze-winged and white-capped Pionus parrots.

The most common Pionus pet readily accessible to avian lovers is the Blue-headed. With a blue cranium sitting atop a predominantly green body it has been noted to be the most popular pet chosen by avian enthusiasts to raise.

The Maximilian which is found in the regions of Central America, the basin of the Amazon as well as Argentina is another one of the most popular pet Pionus in the pet trade. Closely at the Maximilian's heels in terms of popularity would be the White-capped Pionus and the Blue-headed Pionus.

Chapter Ten: Additional Requirements and Summary

It has been observed that most handfed Pionus parrots are a tad quicker in learning the social graces when often mingled with people. It is a lot quieter and is less of a talker compared to other parrots usually favored and kept as pets, but these exact characteristics may also be the reasons why they are more and more looked at to be pets within families. This chapter will include some more additional requirements and a bit of summary to wrap up your Pionus parrot experience and learning.

Quick Summary

Their being quiet can usually be mistaken for shyness or that they are aloof of company but if you give them and yourself time you will understand that these initial traits are shared by most beings that are in unusual and unfamiliar situations. It is in fact a pretty chilled out and easy-going bird who just isn't much of a talker.

Observation has proven, though, Pionus birds are able to learn select phrases and words when raised by owners or trained by people with shriller, higher pitched voices. All in all these little subtly-colored parrots make really good family pets and companions around the house.

Also known as the red vented parrots, Pionus birds are really smart parrots that are generally playful and would welcome interaction with a familiar face once they get to know the individual. There is also something quietly rewarding about gently playing with a Pionus. There is just something about them that brings out the tranquility within you.

They are gracious housemates who are able to integrate themselves easily into the new homes they join. They are curious investigators of anything new as long as they do not feel threatened or in danger. Provide the Pionus parrot with toys and trinkets and they will be happy campers who will quietly go about their day amusing you with little antics.

Speaking of antics, like many birds, the Pionus loves the rain. Give it the taste of life in the wild and set a bird shower for it in its enclosure, aviary or cage. A bird bath is also another good addition to its habitat. Do that and your Pionus parrots will be a joy to behold. As time passes you will notice special traits in your Pionus that will endear them more to the family. Aside from being gentle and generally non-peckers, they are pretty loyal birds who tend to bond with those they interact with frequently. They are even sometimes described as being protective of their humans, most notably expressed by the male Pionus.

Bird Housing, Toys, Playpens and other Equipment

Pionus parrots are quick to adapt to their cage and surroundings making them great companions who integrate well. The majority of most Pionus parrots are housed in cages inside homes, allowed to take a bit of wind under their wings in a bird room, or together with other pionus-friendly birds in an aviary. Bird cages should be spacious enough not too confining. So you want to get one where your pet parrot is be able to feel at home and is comfortable. Aside from housing and perches you will also need dishes for treats, food, and water.

Housing and Bird Cages for Different Species

Due to the general size similarity, an enclosure best suited for a Pionus parrot to house in would be similar to that required by an Amazon parrot. The enclosure must be between 39"- 59" (100-150 cm) tall and must have a floor space of about 23"x 39" (60 x 100 cm). It has been suggested though that optimally a minimum size cage could be 24"x 24"x 32" (62 x 62 x 83 cm). Bar spacing measuring 3/4" is recommended, although 1 inch bar spacing is more suitable for the larger pionus sort.

The enclosure has to have a lot room to allow for lots of movement and don't forget to make space for food dishes, perches, and plenty of playthings. Things your bird can play with could include parrot swings, climbing ropes, bells, chains, and wooden or other bird toys. A playpen is ideal for playtime outside of the cage because it can double up as exercise area for the birds.

Temperatures

Once acclimated, the Pionus can do really good in a breeding or an outdoor aviary but not all of them tolerate cold temperatures. For instance the Dusky Pionus cannot be kept below 50 ° F (10° C) whereas the Bronze-winged Pionus must not be housed where temperatures fall below 41° F (5° C) so be mindful of the kind of pionus you bring home and take stock of your home and how you can outfit it if you are getting either of the two.

There will be a number of factors you will need to pay mind when choosing an outdoor aviary. An aviary outdoors must have parts of it sheltered and protected. You have to be able to get this enclosure heated and cooled when necessary. It should also have an attached flight cage. It is advised that the aviary be at least 6 - 8 feet 12' (180 - 240 cm) long with room to place a perch on either end. The width of the aviary for a pair of birds is not as important and a measure of about 3' - 4' (90 - 120 cm) would be fine.

Remember that anything that will stimulate their minds, give them opportunity to hone their natural skills and allow the bird to play safely are apt and wise additions to promote positive development.

Health Maintenance

Aside from giving birds the proper and balanced nutrition they need in order to maintain good health, cage sanitation and cleanliness follows closely. Most animals that were once healthy only to later develop skin, feather and health conditions were noted to have been housed in poor conditions. Make sure that you maintain the cage by thoroughly cleaning the bowls and water containers, making sure that no food remnants or droppings get into their food. You should individually remove and wash all the toys and perches. The floor should be washed about every other week at the least or when needed. A total disinfecting and hosing down of its cage has to be accomplished at two times in a year whilst replacing fixtures that which have been worn out by use, such as old dishes, perches and toys.

Legal Aspects of Owning

Recent years has been witness to more and more parrot sanctuaries and parrot rescues cropping up which indicate a spike in uninformed and misinformed once-keeper of these relatively quiet parrots. Populations of some of the pionus species have also been affected greatly.

Before making up your mind about acquiring a pionus parrot as a pet, it is crucial for the interested future owner to do extensive research on the bird. It allows the potential pet keeper to become more familiar with national and international trade rules regarding the ownership of pionus parrots.

CITES stands for Convention on International Trade in Endangered Species of Wild Fauna and Flora. It protects parrots by regulating its import, export, and re-export through an international convention authorized through a licensing system. Different species are assigned in different appendix statuses such as Appendix I, II or III etc. These appendices indicate the level of threat to the current population of the bird with consideration to their likely ability to rebound in the wild with legal trade.

Tips of How to Spot a Legit Breeder/Bird

- With so many more parrot species becoming endangered in the wild, even the parrot species not found on the endangered lists are presently protected by the Convention on International Trade in Endangered Species of Wild Fauna and Flora or CITES.

- Purchasing parrots is by no means illegal but the potential keeper guardian will have to follow a set of rules and certain regulations made to avoid and stave off the proliferation of endangered parrots illegally caught in the wild from entering the market.

- Do not forget that the national laws in your home country about owning or breeding these parrots could be different from international rules so it up to you to read up, ask around and familiarize yourself with these regulations. As the potential owner of a pionus parrot or two, it will be up to you to determine regulation details of your own home country.

- All breeding and companion birds they should all be individually are given an identifiable mark or identification device to help recover it should it get lost. Identification will also be useful to assist in the maintenance of genealogical and medical records.

- A lot of breeders attach closed legs bands or rings whilst the chicks are young. Whilst these identification marks or devices may present a measure of risk of entrapment, closed bands are more ideal than no identification at all, most especially for breeding birds.

- Microchips, which are implanted under the skin or into the muscle, are reliable means to identify birds individually. Electronic microchip readers are used to verify identification.

- Tattoos can also be used as a form of identification but typically fade or become illegible with time. Footprints could also be used as a tool in identification.

Glossary of Bird Terms

Addled eggs - These eggs are not viable and will not hatch.

Afterfeather - A structure that projects from the shaft of the feather at the rim of the superior umbilicus.

Allopreening - An act of social grooming amongst birds, in which one bird preens the other or a pair of birds does so mutually.

alternate plumage - The plumage of birds displayed in time for courtship or a breeding season.

Altricial - hatchlings with their eyes closed, and are not capable of leaving the nest on its own, and relies on parents for food.

Alula - a bird's "thumb"

Anisodactylus - a bird foot which has three toes pointing forward and one toe pointing at the back

Anting - a behaviour when birds rub insects, typically ants, on their feathers and skin

Aviculture - captive breeding and raising of birds

Back- exterior area of a bird's upper parts between its mantle and rump

basic plumage - non-breeding plumage

Beak - bill or rostrum

beak trimming - the partial removal of the beak

Belly - the area beneath the chest of a bird

Billing - a tendency of mated pairs that strengthen couple bonding

bird banding - a tag attached to the leg of a bird to enable identification

bird strike - bird/s that impact with planes in flight

Body down - soft, down feathers underneath a birds outer feathers.

Breast - body part between throat and belly

breeding plumage - plumage displayed by birds during breeding season

Brood - offspring birds

brood patch - an area of bare skin well supplied with blood vessels at the surface, and facilitates the transfer of heat to the eggs

Call - bird vocalization intending to serve as warning alarm

Cloaca - birds expel waste from it; other mate by joining cloaca; females lay eggs from this region

contact call - to make known to their kind the location of a bird

Crissum - feathered area between the vent and the tail

cryptic plumage - plumage meant to camouflage birds

definitive plumage - plumage completely developed and fixed

Down - the softest of the birds feathers

Egg - where birds develop until hatched

egg incubation - act of warming the eggs to promote hatching

Eye-ring - visible ring of feathers surrounding a bird's eyes

Feather - distinct outer "garment" covering a birds' body

feather pecking - a behavioural problem when one bird repeatedly pecks at the feathers of another bird

Fledge - a young bird that completely develops its wing muscles and feather suitable for flight

Fledgling - the period when a completely formed young bird ventures out of the nest and learns to take flight

Flight - the act of soaring in the air with the use of wings

Gizzard - specialized stomach organ found in the digestive tract of some birds used to grind up food and aided with grit or stone particles

Gleaning - a bird strategy used to catch insect prey

Grooming - the act of preening and self-cleaning

Iris - coloured outer ring surrounding birds' pupil

Lek - male aggression when in competition for the attention of a female

Mantle - front area of a bird's upper portion found between nape and top back

Migration - seasonal movement of birds

Morph - a polymorphic plumage colour variance between the same species

Moult - a periodic shedding and replacement of feathers

Nail - hard tissue at the tip of a bird's beak

Nares - two holes leading to the nasal cavities in the bird's skull

Nest - a bird's lair and home; where a female lays eggs and roosts

Over-brooding - a phenomenon when birds continue to brood eggs not likely to hatch

Passerine - any bird of the order Passeriformes

Pinioning - the removal of the joint of a bird's wing farthest from the body preventing flight

Plumage - refers to feathers covering a bird as well as pattern, colour and arrangement of feathers

Plumeology - the study of feathers

pre-alternate moult - also known as the prenuptial moult when basic plumage is shed to make way for nuptial plumage

prebasic moult - moult birds go through after breeding season

Precocial - young birds that after hatched has their eyes open

Preening - grooming od feathers in birds

Quill - the main stem of a feather where all structures branch from

Resident - a non-migratory bird

rictal bristles stiff, tapering feathers around the eyes of some birds

Rosette - a found at the corners of the beaks of some birds. A fleshy rosette area

Rump - area of a bird's body between the end of the back and the base of the tail

sexual dimorphism - common occurrence amongst birds in which males and females of a similar sort display different character traits

Song - bird vocalization associated with courtship

Speculum - A patch of typically bright coloured feathers, often iridescent

Sternum - bird's breastbone

Syrinx - the vocal organs of birds

Tail streamers - narrow tips of the tail of some birds

Talon - claw of bird of prey

Teleoptiles - feathers of an adult bird

Throat - body area located between the chin and the upper part of the breast

Thigh - body part between knee and trunk of the bird's body

Vent - the outer opening of the cloaca

Wings - The bird's forelimbs that are the essential to flight

Wingspan - distance between wings from one wing tip to the other

Index

A

accessories..14, 44, 45, 84, 130, 140, 148

animal movement license...52

Aspergillosis...127, 128, 129, 130

Asymptomatic...123, 125, 126

Aviary...56, 57

B

behavior..11, 40, 41, 137

breeder...13,49,53,54,55,82,110,114,116

breeding............................. 11, 12, 109, 110, 111, 112, 113, 114, 115, 141, 149

brooding...114

C

cage...............................140, 43, 44, 45, 47, 84, 85, 86, 87, 88, 89, 92, 99, 130, 137, 140, 146

calcium...100, 101, 141

CITES...50,51,52

clutch...11, 54, 111, 113, 114, 142

cost 39, 40, 43, 44, 45, 46, 47, 48

cyanosis..128

cuttlebone..100, 140, 141

D

diagnosis 126, 129, 131,133, 134, 135

diet 12, 46, 54, 89, 90, 93, 94, 95, 99, 100, 130, 139, 141, 150

diseases 13, 52, 94, 99, 113, 119, 120, 121, 135

dishes..44, 88, 89, 130, 140, 148

DNA...11, 110, 131, 132

droppings...89, 113, 136

E

E-Coli...11, 12, 99, 100, 111, 113, 114, 115, 139, 142

eggs...42, 85, 113, 127, 130

environment .... .17,37,39,44,69,70,72,82

eyes...20, 21, 82, 121, 125, 128, 137

F

family...10, 12, 14, 139

feather...9, 10, 40, 42, 82, 91, 99, 131, 136, 137

feeding...44, 46, 93, 94, 95, 130

female...11, 109, 110, 111, 114, 142

food....................46, 47, 48, 84, 86, 88, 89, 90, 94, 102, 136, 140, 141, 142, 150

fruits...46, 90, 93, 97, 99, 102, 130, 141

G

genus...16, 17, 18, 25, 26, 27, 28, 29

Great Britain...50, 52, 53, 78, 146, 147

grooming...43, 45, 91, 106, 107, 140

H

habitat...12, 27, 85, 137, 139

handling 91, 103

hatching 114, 142

health.................................52, 54, 82, 86, 88, 89, 120, 123, 131, 135, 137

history...7,23,55

hygiene..45, 91

I

illness...95, 121, 123, 127, 135

immune system..95, 122, 123, 127, 130

incubation...11, 12, 111, 114, 115, 139, 142

infection..............120, 121, 122, 123, 124, 125, 128, 129, 132, 133, 134, 135, 137

initial costs...43

L

lay...142

license..52

lifespan...2, 11, 12, 139

longevity..82

M

male..109, 110

mating...111

maturity 11, 12, 110, 111, 114, 139, 142

N

nails...91, 103, 106, 107, 130, 131

nest.. 111, 113, 114, 115, 140, 142

nesting..113, 114

nutrients...89, 90, 93, 94, 95

nutritional...46, 93, 94, 141

needs...45, 46, 47, 84, 85, 86, 88, 91, 94, 99, 131

O

oil..91, 143

order...12, 85, 94, 112, 139

P

Pacheco's Disease...126

parrots.................................2, 3, 8, 9, 11, 42, 45, 47, 90, 92, 94, 97, 102

PBFD virus...130

pellet...46, 89, 90, 94, 95, 99, 140

perches...44, 86, 88, 89, 130, 140, 142, 143

permit...49, 51, 52

pet store...13, 45, 46, 53, 54, 89, 107

prevention...119, 130, 132, 137

Psittacosis..125, 126

Q

quick..12, 14, 15, 18, 105

R

reproduction..11, 110, 111, 113

respiratory..................................91, 121, 122, 125, 127, 128, 129, 133, 137, 143

S

seeds...................11, 12, 46, 89, 90, 93, 94, 96, 97, 103, 130, 139, 141, 143, 150

seed mix...89, 140, 141

sexing...11, 110, 141

sexually dimorphic...11, 12, 110, 139, 141

species...9, 13, 106, 115, 120, 124, 127, 129, 130, 142

symptoms..................119, 120, 121, 122, 123, 124, 125, 126, 127, 131, 133, 134

T

taming..104

training...102, 103, 105, 106, 143

temperature 91, 92, 111, 140

toys 35, 43, 44, 45, 47, 89, 140, 142, 148

Treats..46, 90, 102

treatment...........................47, 101, 120, 121, 122, 124, 129, 130, 132, 134

types...............................9, 14, 18, 35, 36, 37, 39, 41, 42, 47, 88, 90, 94, 141

U

United States.....................................13, 26, 27, 50, 51, 52, 55, 116, 146

V

vegetables 46, 90, 95, 99, 130, 141, 127

ventilation 127

veterinarian 91, 97, 99, 107, 108, 135, 137, 143

virus. 120, 121, 122, 123, 124, 126, 127, 131, 132

W

water 86, 87, 88, 89, 90, 91, 101

wild 37, 42, 50, 88, 93, 94, 106, 113

wingspan 11, 12, 19, 20, 21, 25, 28, 31, 32

Photo Credits

Page 1 Photo by user Bernard Dupont via Flickr.com
https://www.flickr.com/photos/berniedup/31408797720/

Page 10 Photo by user Anna Hesser via Flickr.com
https://www.flickr.com/photos/annahesser/6381086517/

Page 15 Photo by user Travis Wise via Flickr.com
https://www.flickr.com/photos/photographingtravis/1502626
0460/

Page 25 Photo by user Arley Vargas via Flickr.com
https://www.flickr.com/photos/125236336@N05/35550530793
/

Page 34 Photo by user Tony Morris via Flickr.com
https://www.flickr.com/photos/tonymorris/6775272507/

Page 41 Photo by user UCI UC Irvine via Flickr.com
https://www.flickr.com/photos/ucirvine/23350113821/

Page 53 Photo by user Anna Hesser via Flickr.com
https://www.flickr.com/photos/annahesser/6463314149/

Page 59 Photo by user Arley Vargas via Flickr.com
https://www.flickr.com/photos/125236336@N05/35962151290
/

Page 76 Photo by user Rüdiger Stehn via Flickr.com
https://www.flickr.com/photos/rstehn/16613765293/

Page 83 Photo by user Tracy Bridges via Flickr.com
https://www.flickr.com/photos/yubunug/2526213838/

References

"About Pionus Parrots – Pionus Parrot Care" Animal-world.com

http://animal-world.com/encyclo/birds/pionus/PionusProfile.htm

"Bronze-winged Pionus" Animal-world.com

http://animal-world.com/encyclo/birds/pionus/bronzewgpion.php

"Caging & Toys" PionusOnline.com

http://www.pionusonline.com/caging_and_toys.htm

"Dusky Pionus" Animal-world.com

http://animal-world.com/encyclo/birds/pionus/duskypion.php

"Feeding Guide for Pionus Parrots" Second-Opinion-Doc.com

http://www.second-opinion-doc.com/feeding-guide-for-pionus-parrots.html

"How to Choose a Pionus Parrot" Wikihow.com

http://www.wikihow.pet/Choose-a-Pionus-Parrot

"How to Tame Your Wild or Aggressive Parrot
Dealing with Unwanted Behaviors in Your Pet Parrot"
2ndchance.info

http://www.2ndchance.info/tameparrot.htm

"Maximilian's Pionus" Animal-world.com

http://animal-
world.com/encyclo/birds/pionus/maxipion.php

"Nutrition" PionusParrot.com

http://www.pionusparrot.com/Nutrition.htm

"Pionus" Wikipedia.org

https://en.wikipedia.org/wiki/Pionus

"Pionus Menstruus" PetEducation.com

http://www.peteducation.com/article.cfm?c=15+1840&aid=23
34

"Pionus Parrot" Lafeber.com

https://lafeber.com/pet-birds/species/pionus-parrots/

"Pionus parrots are beautiful, quiet, sweet birds" Parrot-
and-Conure-World.com

http://www.parrot-and-conure-world.com/pionus.html

"Pionus Parrots Feeding" Purrsngrrs.com

http://purrsngrrs.com/pionus-parrots-feeding/

"Pionus Parrots Training" Purrsngrrs.com

http://purrsngrrs.com/pionus-parrots-training/

"Pionus Parrots' Wild Habits" Petcha.com

https://www.petcha.com/pionus-parrots-wild-habits/

"Plum-crowned Parrots" BeautyofBirds.com

https://www.beautyofbirds.com/plumcrownedparrots.html

"Positively Appealing Pionus Parrots"

https://www.petcha.com/positively-appealing-pionus-parrots/

"Red-billed Pionus Parrots" BeautyofBirds.com

https://www.beautyofbirds.com/redbilledpionusparrots.html

"White-crowned Pionus" Animal-world.com

http://animal-world.com/encyclo/birds/pionus/whtpion.php

"White-headed Pionus or Speckle-faced Parrot" BeautyofBirds.com

https://www.beautyofbirds.com/whiteheadedparrots.html

Feeding Baby
Cynthia Cherry
978-1941070000

Axolotl
Lolly Brown
978-0989658430

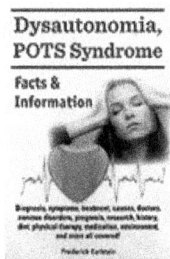

Dysautonomia, POTS
Syndrome
Frederick Earlstein
978-0989658485

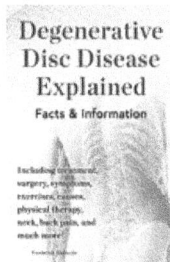

Degenerative Disc
Disease Explained
Frederick Earlstein
978-0989658485

Sinusitis, Hay Fever,
Allergic Rhinitis Explained
Frederick Earlstein
978-1941070024

Wicca
Riley Star
978-1941070130

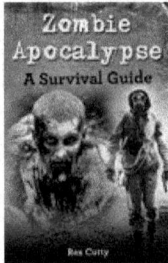

Zombie Apocalypse
Rex Cutty
978-1941070154

Capybara
Lolly Brown
978-1941070062

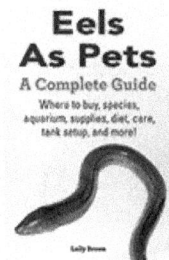

Eels As Pets
Lolly Brown
978-1941070167

Scabies and Lice Explained
Frederick Earlstein
978-1941070017

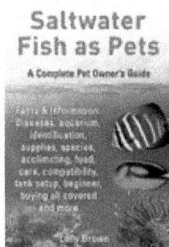

Saltwater Fish As Pets
Lolly Brown
978-0989658461

Torticollis Explained
Frederick Earlstein
978-1941070055

Kennel Cough
Lolly Brown
978-0989658409

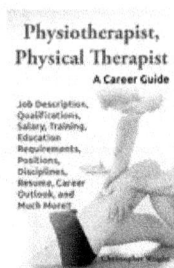

Physiotherapist, Physical
Therapist
Christopher Wright
978-0989658492

Rats, Mice, and Dormice
As Pets
Lolly Brown
978-1941070079

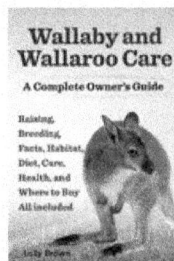

Wallaby and Wallaroo Care
Lolly Brown
978-1941070031

Bodybuilding Supplements
Explained
Jon Shelton
978-1941070239

Demonology
Riley Star
978-19401070314

Pigeon Racing
Lolly Brown
978-1941070307

Dwarf Hamster
Lolly Brown
978-1941070390

Cryptozoology
Rex Cutty
978-1941070406

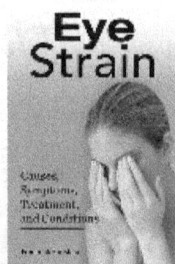

Eye Strain
Frederick Earlstein
978-1941070369

Inez The Miniature Elephant
Asher Ray
978-1941070353

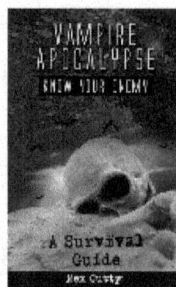

Vampire Apocalypse
Rex Cutty
978-1941070321

www.ingramcontent.com/pod-product-compliance
Lightning Source LLC
Chambersburg PA
CBHW052114090426
42741CB00009B/1806